'An informed and essential guide to Luther's life and theology through the presentation of the 95 theses that changed the course of church history. Brownell not only expounds the significance of that document in the context of the 16th century but helps the reader to apply it to our present-day situation. The conviction that lies at the heart of the book is that the Protestant Reformation has many lessons to teach to Reformational churches as they seek to remain faithful to the Gospel of Jesus Christ in the midst of the many challenges they face, both internally and externally. A simple yet profound book to be accompanied by in the celebrations of the 5th centenary of the Reformation.'

Leonardo De Chirico, lecturer in Historical Theology (IFED, Padova, Italy) and director of the Reformanda Initiative.

'Each generation of to the great events o like towering mount  to be emboldened to seek spiritual own day. The start of the Protestant Reformation of the 16th century is one such great event. Kenneth Brownell captures that historic moment in this admirably readable little book. He then proposes

"9.5 theses" that challenge us to follow in the footsteps of the Reformer Martin Luther to recover Reformational (i.e. true biblical) Christianity today. What will our response be?'

Conrad Mbewe, Pastor of Kabwata Baptist Church and Chancellor of the African Christian University, Lusaka, Zambia.

'Kenneth Brownell brilliantly summarises what Luther stood for 500 years ago as well as updating his ideas for 500 years later - today.'

Jeremy Marshall, Chairman of Christianity Explored, Pastor Training International and Christian Books Worldwide and treasurer of London Seminary.

LUTHER
AND THE ~~95~~ 9.5 THESES

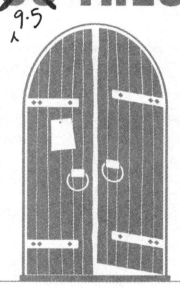

By→ **KENNETH BROWNELL**

LUTHER

AND THE ~~95~~ THESES

9.5

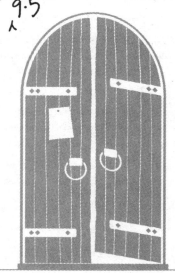

By → **KENNETH BROWNELL**

10 Publishing

a division of **10** of those.com

First published in Great Britain in 2017

British Library Cataloguing in Publication Data
A record for this book is available from the British Library

ISBN: 978-1-9-1127-236-6

Designed and typeset by Pete Barnsley (CreativeHoot)

Printed in Denmark by Nørhaven

10Publishing, a division of 10ofthose.com
Unit C, Tomlinson Road, Leyland, PR25 2DY, England

Email: info@10ofthose.com
Website: www.10ofthose.com

CONTENTS

INTRODUCTION

On 31 October 1517 Martin Luther posted the now famous 95 Theses on the door of the Castle Church in Wittenberg and changed the world. Yet he didn't intend to change the world but only to begin a debate about what he considered a corrupt practice in the church. This book is first about how Luther reached the point of posting his 95 Theses and why his actions were so significant. In the opening two chapters I will give an overview of Luther's life before and after 1517. Second, I will then propose my own theses – 9.5 of them rather than Luther's 95 – for the recovery of Reformational Christianity today.[1]

I use the expression Reformational Christianity

rather than Protestant or evangelical Christianity because the currency of the words 'Protestant' and 'evangelical' has sadly become so devalued. Reformational Christianity is simply orthodox Christianity as shaped by the great concerns of the Reformation. These concerns are summed up by the famous *solas* or 'alones' of the Reformation – salvation is by grace alone (*sola gratia* in Latin), through faith alone (*sola fide*), from Scripture alone (*sola scriptura*), in Christ alone (*solus Christus*) and to the glory of God alone (*soli deo gloria*).[2] Remembering what happened in Wittenberg in 1517 and its aftermath should stir up in us a desire for the recovery of the Christianity of the Reformation.

Such a recovery is desperately needed here in the United Kingdom, in Europe and around the world, where we are all too aware of the decline of Christianity. In some measure this has been because of what is called secularisation, as religion in general and Christianity in particular have been pushed out of the public square to the margins of society and into the sphere of private life. There is a lot of debate about the nature of secularisation and why it has happened, but there is no doubt that in the UK and Europe the institutional church is very weak as a result. The old denominations, many of them with their origins in the Reformation, are declining.

Sadly, in addition to secularisation, another large part of the problem has been liberal theology, which has robbed churches in many older denominations of the biblical gospel. While happily inside and outside these denominations there are congregations in varying degrees of spiritual health which are faithful to the gospel, they are relatively few compared to the population at large. Equally it is true that the immigration of many people from countries with large numbers of evangelical Christians has led to many new churches and new life in old ones. However, many of these churches have been blighted with the prosperity gospel and its crass materialism.

Even in many evangelical churches unaffected by liberalism or the prosperity gospel, preaching and teaching from the Bible is in a poor state and often treated as a Cinderella compared to other things considered more important. Then, of course, there is the fact that the Roman Catholic

Church is still essentially the same today as it was in Luther's day, if not in some ways worse.

In short, while our circumstances are very different from those of Luther in the late 16th century, for the reasons above, and others, the need for the Christianity that emerged from the Reformation is still as great if not greater.

PART 1

A SHORT OVERVIEW OF MARTIN LUTHER'S LIFE

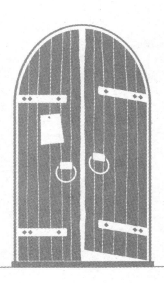

1

HOW AND WHY DID MARTIN LUTHER COME TO POST HIS 95 THESES IN 1517?

Who exactly was this Martin Luther who posted his now famous theses?[3] He was at the time a professor of theology in the relatively new university of Wittenberg. Wittenberg was not, compared to some other German cities, a very important place and at this stage in his life Luther was not a very important person.

He was born in 1483 in Eisleben, where in a curious turn of providence he would die 63 years later in 1546. His family moved the year after he was born to Mansfeld, where his father, Hans, worked in the mines and eventually came to manage several of them. Moderately well off, Hans wanted his son to become a lawyer and to that end paid for him to attend good schools in Mansfeld, Magdeburg and Eisenach. A precociously bright boy, young Martin matriculated at the University of Erfurt, where he began to study law.

However, having earned two degrees, Luther changed course and decided to become a monk in 1505. What convinced him was famously a frightening thunderstorm. On his way home from university he was so terrified during the storm that he cried out to St Anne for protection and vowed that if he survived he would take the monastic vow, which he then did. Hans was furious since he had great ambitions for his son, but Martin was determined. He entered the Order of Augustinian Hermits and in 1507 celebrated his first mass, which his father refused to attend. Years later, when no longer a monk but something of a celebrity preacher, Martin wrote to his father and apologised for his behaviour but said that nevertheless God had overruled his disobedience for the sake of the gospel.[4] What Hans thought of this we don't know, although they seemed to have been reconciled before he died.

Having devoted himself to the monastic life, Luther began to climb the theological academic ladder. In part this suited his inclination to study, but it was also with the encouragement of his confessor, Johann von Staupitz, who saw it as a way to divert Luther from his preoccupation with the state of his soul. Luther simply could not find assurance that he was in a state of grace in spite of the most assiduous use of the church's penitential and devotional practices. As Luther wrote about this time, 'I hoped I might find peace of conscience with fasts, prayer, vigils, with which I miserably afflicted my body; but the more I sweated it out like this, the less peace and tranquillity I knew.'[5] A visit to Rome on behalf of his order didn't help to ease his conscience. Later in life Luther used that visit as ammunition against his Catholic adversaries, but at the time he was more concerned for his own soul than the state of the church. Though Staupitz was a wise, gentle and patient counsellor, as well as a friend, his efforts did little to assure Luther either.

However, academic work was a practical outlet at which Luther excelled, as was administrative work for the order of which he became a district visitor. By 1511 Luther was transferred to the University in Wittenberg, where he gained his doctorate in theology the following year. His speciality was the Bible, on which he began to lecture: the Psalms in 1513, Romans in 1515, Galatians in 1516 and Hebrews in 1517. As we'll see that was very significant. Luther was also appointed the principal preacher in the Castle Church.

At the same time as Luther was settling into his academic career, his attention was drawn to the sale of indulgences. These were part of a very elaborate and complicated system for dealing with the sins of Christians that the church had developed over preceding centuries. At the heart of this penitential system was the sacrament of penance.[6] This was comprised of four parts: the individual's contrition or sorrow for their sin; the person's confession of this sin to a priest; satisfaction to God or recompense for sin gained by an individual undertaking certain works; and a priest's absolution for their sin.

As is evident in the 95 Theses, initially Luther didn't have a problem with this penitential system as such. His problem was with what was being demanded of Christians for the satisfaction of their sins through the purchase of indulgences. An indulgence is basically a cancellation by the church of the satisfaction required of Christians if they are to be forgiven. In preparing his theses Luther had discovered that the current practice of the church was not what it had been in earlier centuries. Then indulgences had been things required by a confessor for a penitent to do in order to make satisfaction for his or her sins, and they were seen to work by drawing on the treasury of merit of Christ and the saints that the church administered through the penitential system. However by the early 16th century indulgences had evolved to become the means by which the church claimed to remit or cancel the punishments in purgatory of Christians that were owing when they died, and they were obtained by paying money to the church. In the years leading up to 1517 Luther was coming to see that something was wrong about all this.

What brought things to an explosive head was the way indulgences were being sold in regions neighbouring Saxony where Wittenberg was located. The main culprit was a monk named Johan Tetzel, who had been employed by Albrecht, the Archbishop of Mainz and the senior ecclesiastical official in that part of the world. Tetzel went around many towns and cities in Germany selling indulgences that were not merely intended to let purchasers off doing penance but to get them or those they had been purchased for out of purgatory altogether. His indulgences promised total forgiveness of sins after death. And in selling these indulgences Tetzel was a master salesman. His entrance into a town was a big public event with a loud and colourful procession attended by all the local bigwigs. He famously used the jingle that Luther would quote in his theses: 'Every time a coin in the coffer rings, a soul from purgatory springs,' though Luther himself only heard about all this by hearsay.

Frederick III, the Elector of Saxony and thus the local political power, had forbidden Tetzel to preach in his territories. This wasn't because Frederick objected to indulgences, but because he didn't want money diverted from the church in Wittenberg which housed his very extensive collection of relics and which attracted large numbers of pilgrims. (This would later prove to be ironic since Frederick would become the protector of Luther, the man who would do more than anything else to destroy the system of devotion focused on relics.) Likewise in 1517 what concerned Luther was not Frederick's relics but the way Tetzel was abusing indulgences in order to sell them. What grieved Luther was that people from around Wittenberg were travelling to places outside Frederick's domain to purchase these indulgences.

If Luther's problem with indulgences was only one rogue salesman, nothing much would have probably come of his protest. However it was a far bigger problem than that. Albrecht had employed Tetzel because he needed money. Albrecht, the younger son of a prominent aristocratic family, had become Bishop of Magdeburg. Yet soon after that the far more ecclesiastically important and politically powerful position of the Archbishopric of Mainz had become vacant. In order to obtain this title Albrecht was required to pay a lot of money, which he had borrowed from the Fugger banking family. But where was he to find the money to repay the loan?

Happily for him Pope Leo X also needed money for the rebuilding of St Peter's Basilica in Rome. He had undertaken to reconstruct this in the magnificence that we can still see today, employing Michelangelo, Raphael, Bramante and a host of other artists and architects. Yet this cost a lot of cash, of which the papacy was short. So in 1515 the pope had decreed a plenary indulgence, that is an indulgence that remitted all a person's sins, for the purpose of raising funds for the rebuilding project.

In order to sell this plenary indulgence in the regions within Albrecht's jurisdiction the pope brokered a deal with him in which they would split the proceeds 50-50. It was a win-win situation for everyone concerned – the pope and Albrecht obtained their money, Tetzel was paid for his role and had a lot of fun in the process, and those people who bought the plenary indulgence believed they could go straight to heaven when they died or from purgatory if they had died already.

Everyone was happy – except for Martin Luther. Luther knew nothing of the pope and Albrecht's deal. His concern was that the sale of indulgences in this way meant that people could escape dealing with sin and the judgment of God, and he considered this to be to the peril of their souls. He began early in 1517 to preach about indulgences, gently chiding his hearers in Wittenberg for travelling to towns outside Electoral Saxony. In one sermon he expressed his concern that indulgences 'work against grace', by which he meant inner repentance. 'You see,' he said, '... how dangerous a thing the preaching of indulgences is, which teaches a mutilated grace, namely to flee satisfaction and punishment.'[7] At this stage Luther still believed that sins in the lives of Christians had to be dealt with according to the church's penitential system, which included doing penance to make satisfaction for them. The problem as he perceived it was that the indulgences Tetzel was selling undermined that. Luther wasn't alone in raising questions about the abuse of indulgences in his sermons – his mentor, Staupitz, as well as others did so too. Yet in the light of what happened next it is Luther's preaching that stands out.[8]

Alongside his preaching Luther began to investigate the history of indulgences by looking at ancient documents. In this he used the approach of the New Learning style that had emerged from the Renaissance, encapsulated in its motto *ad fontes*, meaning 'to the sources'. New Learning involved going back to the ancient Greek and Roman classics and carrying out careful philological study, whereby the language and structure of the literary texts were studied. The university in Wittenberg was a centre of the New Learning and Luther was a passionate advocate.

As well as examining the church's documents related to indulgences, Luther also went back to the works of the church fathers – ancient Christian theologians – and beyond them to Scripture. His approach was not to accept the authority given to some writings by the church but to give priority to older writings over more recent ones in line with the approach of New

Learning. He discovered that what was being preached and practised was different from that of the early church. More importantly he was beginning to see that indulgences were not in line with the teaching of the Bible.

He was helped in this latter conclusion by developments in the study of the Bible, his area of study and teaching. The New Learning emphasised knowing Hebrew and Greek in order to read the Bible in its original languages. Luther had been doing this, with the particular aid of the publication in the previous year of the Greek New Testament by Desiderius Erasmus, a Dutch scholar. This work also included in parallel columns the Vulgate, the official Latin version of the Bible, which had been translated by Jerome in the fifth century. From comparing the two versions Luther discovered that penance as understood by the church was not repentance as taught in Scripture. Thus the basis for the theology of penance was not the words of Jesus. An example of this can be seen in how the two different versions render Jesus' words in Matthew 4:17. Whereas the Vulgate translates the relevant words as *poenitentium agite*, meaning 'do penance', the Greek text should be translated in English as 'repent'.

Luther was thus beginning to understand that repentance was something completely different from penance. His comprehension of this was further helped by his preparation for lecturing on the Bible. As an exponent of New Learning he was engaging with the text of Scripture. Then, as he encountered the word of God, his thinking was changing, not only in relation to indulgences but in many other areas too.

Driven by this understanding Luther finally decided to do something about the scandal of Tetzel's indulgence sale. He wanted to begin an academic debate about them, and posting a series of theses to this effect was the customary practice for a professor like Luther. Moreover in Wittenberg the door of the Castle Church was the place to post a debate along with other public notices.

So on 31 October 1517 Luther nailed his 95 Theses on the main door of the Castle Church in which he expressed his concerns about indulgences. However, significant as this event is in retrospect, it is not entirely clear what happened on the day itself. It doesn't seem to have been the dramatic event it is sometimes portrayed to have been. If it was so significant to Luther, it is strange that he never commented on it, as he did many other things of importance. He was a great talker but not once in his *Table Talk* is it mentioned. The first reference to the event comes in the preface to *Luther's Latin Works* that Philip Melanchthon, Luther's younger colleague and associate, wrote in 1546, four months after Luther's death, and even then it is only as an aside. While Melanchthon was in a good position to know if Luther had actually posted the theses, and may well have been told about it, he hadn't been there at the time, only arriving in Wittenberg in 1519 to take up his post as the new professor of Greek. For this reason some have suggested that the theses were never actually posted publicly.

However, a factor supporting the notion that the theses were indeed posted on the door was their timing. The following day was the feast of All Saints, when many people came to the church to venerate the relics there. By posting his theses on the door through which many would pass, Luther would be making a very pointed and public announcement. Then, as already mentioned, for a professor like Luther to initiate an academic debate, he needed to do so publicly, and the door of the Castle Church was the place to do so. It is very likely then that Luther did actually post his theses but that it was more a matter of course rather than being important in itself, in spite of the significance it has gained in retrospect in the Protestant imagination.

Without a doubt what is far more important than where Luther nailed his theses is that on the same day he sent them along with a letter to Albrecht of Mainz. This more than anything else sparked the flame that became the Reformation fire. Luther was unaware that both Albrecht and Pope Leo X were deeply mired in the indulgences scandal and wouldn't welcome his interference. Albrecht sent Luther's theses to the local theological faculty in Mainz and to the pope in Rome. Before long both condemned what they read and Luther's quarrel with the church began in earnest. At the same time the 95 Theses were almost immediately printed and distributed all over Germany, and very soon

Luther had become a household name not only throughout Germany but also across Europe. Unexpectedly the Reformation had begun.

But what about the content of the 95 Theses themselves? At first glance they are somewhat underwhelming. As a long series of terse propositions for an academic debate they don't exactly get the heart beating faster. There are a few good turns of phrase but most of the theses are about arcane aspects of the doctrine and practice of indulgences. To Protestants the theses in fact seem somewhat un-Protestant – as a still loyal son of the Roman Catholic Church, Luther affirmed his belief in the pope, penance, and indulgences, and had nothing to say about justification by faith or other distinctive doctrines of Protestantism. Yet we need to remember that when he wrote his theses Luther's theology was very much still taking shape, although it would quickly become identifiably Protestant in the next few years. Later in life Luther would look back and admit how ignorant he was at this stage. But just as the Magna Carta proved instrumental in protecting basic liberties in England, the 95 Theses contained the seeds of what became

Reformational Christianity. Understood in the light of what subsequently happened, Luther's 95 Theses were fundamental in establishing the essential elements of Reformational Christianity.

WHAT HAPPENED TO LUTHER AFTER 1517?

In the months after October 1517 Luther increasingly understood that what was at stake in the controversy he had started was far more than the abuse of indulgences. Tetzel came back with his own theses defending indulgences, to which Luther responded, but by then the controversy was already being taken to a wider and higher level. In March 1518 Luther published his *Sermon on Indulgences and Grace* with the aim of informing the general public about the issue. It became an instant bestseller. Then in May he published his *Explanations of the Ninety-Five Theses*.

By now the church was taking Luther's challenge seriously. In October he was summoned to appear before Cardinal Cajetan in Augsburg and ordered to recant his views, which he refused to do. The following year he engaged in a public debate in Leipzig with the German theologian Johan Eck, who had attacked Luther's theses in his own publication, *Obelisci*. As part of the discussion Luther denied the supreme authority of the popes and church councils.

Amidst the controversy – and indeed because of it – Luther was deepening his understanding of the Bible and its message of salvation by grace alone. The breakthrough came in 1519 when, while studying Paul's Letter to the Romans and specifically 1:17, Luther discovered that the righteousness of God was not something demanded of people so that they could merit salvation but what he graciously gave them in Jesus Christ though faith alone. Previously Luther hated the phrase 'the righteousness of God' because of the way it was commonly understood. Yet, as he recalled not long before he died, when writing the preface to his *Latin Works* in 1545:

For my case was this: however irreproachable my life as a monk, I felt myself in the presence of God to be a sinner with a most unquiet conscience, nor could I believe him to be appeased by the satisfaction I could offer. I did not love – nay, I hated this just God who punishes sinners, and if not with silent blasphemy, at least with huge murmuring.

But then everything changed:

At last, God being merciful, as I meditated day and night on the relation of the words 'the righteousness of God is revealed in it,' as it is written, and 'the just shall live by faith,' I began to understand [the] 'justice of God' as that by which the just lives by the grace of God, namely faith; and this sentence, 'the righteousness of God is revealed,' to refer to a passive righteousness, by which the merciful God justifies us by faith, as it is written, 'the just lives by faith.' This straightaway made me feel as though I had been reborn, and as though I had entered through open gates into paradise itself. From that moment, I saw the whole face of Scripture in a new light ... And now, where I had once hated the phrase, 'the righteousness of God,' I began to love and extol it as the sweetest of phrases, so that this passage in Paul became the very gate of paradise to me. [9]

In the years to come, his evangelical theology and programme for Reformation was forged in the crucible of debate in both public disputations and in print, and the prospect of martyrdom was always a possibility. In 1520 Luther published three of his greatest books:

1. *Address to the Christian Nobility of the German Nation*, in which Luther called on the princes of Germany to reform the church since the Roman Curia, the church's central government, were not. Here Luther explained what it meant for every Christian to be a priest.

2. *On the Babylonian Captivity of the Church*, in which Luther used the Old Testament image of Israel's exile in Babylon to show

how the papal church had misused the Bible in order to make Christians subject to it. In this book Luther examined the sacraments of the Roman Catholic Church. The church taught that there were seven sacraments and considered these to be visible signs and a means of receiving God's grace. In contrast Luther redefined them and reduced them to just two: baptism and the Lord's Supper.

3. *On the Freedom of a Christian*, in which Luther got to the heart of the Christian life as shaped by his new understanding of justification by faith alone. Though a small book, Luther stated, 'It contains the whole of Christian life in a brief form'. In it he memorably said, 'A Christian is a perfectly free lord of all, subject to none' and 'a perfectly dutiful servant of all, subject to all'. In other words, Christians, who have been justified through faith alone in Christ, have been set free from all that once enslaved them to serve others in love under the Lordship of Jesus Christ.

Over the coming years Luther wrote many other books, large and small, as well as publishing many of his sermons. Utilising the relatively new technology of the printing press, he became a bestselling author. At the same time the church authorities continued their stance: they were not going to take lying down what Luther was saying against them publicly and in print.

The relationship between Luther and the Roman Catholic Church had taken another dramatic turn in 1520, the year Luther wrote three of his most influential books. A papal bull (an official church proclamation) had been issued, giving him 60 days to recant his views or else warning Luther that he risked excommunication. Luther's response was to publicly burn the bull. Therefore the following year he was duly excommunicated.

That same year the Holy Roman Emperor, Charles V, summoned Luther to an imperial diet or assembly in Worms, Germany to explain himself. Luther refused again to recant his views, famously saying that his conscience was bound by the word of God and – though this has since been disputed by some – adding, 'Here I stand. I can do no other.' A few weeks later, in May 1521, Charles V proclaimed his verdict in his Edict of Worms: Luther was condemned as a heretic and declared an outlaw. His literature was banned, his arrest was demanded and it was prohibited for anyone to give him food and shelter.

However, Luther had left town before this declaration. He had been promised safe conduct but his friends were not so sure about this. Therefore his protector Frederick III, the Elector of Saxony, arranged for Luther to be 'kidnapped' on his way back to Wittenberg and disguised as 'Knight George'. He was then secreted away to Wartburg Castle, where he was hidden for almost a year. It was there that Luther began his monumental work of translating the Bible into German. His German translation of the New Testament was published in 1522, and together with the help of others the translation of the Old Testament was finally finished in 1534.

Yet in 1522 Luther returned to Wittenberg because of the unsettled situation in the town. In his absence his university and pastoral colleague Andreas Karlstadt had taken reforming the church in a more radical direction than Luther felt wise or even in some cases right, and his reforms had led to numerous disturbances. Luther consequently rescinded some of Karlstadt's reforms and settled back into life there as a professor and pastor.

In 1525 one of the biggest changes in Luther's life happened when he married Katharina von Bora. Katharina had been a nun but, like many others, wished to leave her order having read Luther's criticism of the whole monastical system. Luther thought it far better to be living for God in the outside world. Yet Katharina and a group of other nuns were unable to leave freely, so they requested the help of Luther, which resulted in 1523 in them being smuggled out of the convent in barrels by a fish merchant!

Luther had long criticised vows of celibacy on biblical grounds and other formerly celibate priests and nuns had married. Nevertheless he personally had never expected to marry and his marriage took many by surprise. Yet the marriage was a huge success even if Luther was not the easiest of men to live with. Their home was the Black Cloister, Luther's former Augustinian monastery, which had been given to him by the new Elector, John the Steadfast.

There Katharina managed a large household. She bore six children but in addition to them their home included many students whom she had to feed at the meals where Luther held forth on a range of subjects, as recorded in his *Table Talk*. To make ends meet she presided over a farm and ran a brewery. It is for very good reason that Katharina has been called the 'mother of the Reformation', not only because of the help she gave to Luther but also by her being a model of a Protestant wife.

Luther revelled in marriage and family life. Their first child, Hans, was born in 1526. Luther was particularly devoted to his daughter Magdalena, who was born in 1529 and of whom he once said that she had more theology in her little finger than all the bishops in Rome, but tragically she died in 1542. Music-making was a big aspect of family life with Luther playing, singing and teaching new hymns he wrote.

Over the next decades Luther continued his work locally as a pastor and professor as well as more widely in the church, reforming its structures and liturgy. He was also called upon to advise and arbitrate between Protestant political leaders as well as being involved in many disputations with other Protestant church leaders. Sadly there was not unity on a number of issues, particularly that of the Lord's Supper. Luther believed that Christ was really present in the bread and wine, while others, most notably Huldrych Zwingli in Zurich, taught that the elements were merely reminders of the death of Jesus.

Luther felt so strongly on many of these matters that relationships with other reformers were often strained to breaking point. While there was a very generous and gentle side to Luther, he was also a fierce controversialist who could use very strong and often crude language in debate. One aspect of him that is especially hard for people today to understand is the language he used about the Jews – if not anti-Semitic it gets very close to being so. Though this may be in part because Jews hadn't responded to the Reformation by acknowledging Jesus as their Messiah, that was still no excuse; in this regard Luther seems to have reflected the prejudices of his culture.

The end came in 1546. Luther hadn't been keeping in the best of health but, against the advice of Katharina among others, insisted on travelling in the winter to Eisleben, where he had been born, to arbitrate in a dispute between local nobility. He took two of his sons with him. The journey proved hard and shortly before they arrived, Luther collapsed. He was brought to the house where he was to stay and attended by local doctors as his sons and others stood watch. Over the next few days he was able to see people but on 16 February his condition deteriorated. The following evening his friend Justus Jonas asked him, 'Do you want to die standing firm on Christ and the doctrine you have taught?' Luther answered, 'Yes,' and then added, 'We are beggars. This is true.' Shortly afterwards Luther died. He died as a beggar but knowing that his salvation was wholly due to God and his grace in Jesus Christ, and not due to anything Luther had done.

PART 2

MY 9.5 THESES FOR THE RECOVERY OF REFORMATIONAL CHRISTIANITY

– BASED ON MARTIN LUTHER'S 95 THESES

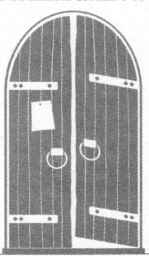

THE STRUCTURE OF THE 95 THESES

What I intend to do for the rest of the book is to propose 9.5 theses for the church today that are drawn from Martin Luther's 95 Theses. I will do this by highlighting some of his theses. In this way I hope we can see how the seeds of the Reformation were sown in those 95 Theses and appreciate how it grew from them. But I also want us to see how Luther's theses can help identify what is needed for the recovery of Reformational Christianity today.

Before we go any further I need to say something about the structure of the 95

Theses. In presenting his theses Luther didn't simply list them randomly but rather followed the customary structure of a proposal for an academic debate.[10] The 95 Theses are arranged as follows:

- The theses begin with an **exordium** or short preface in which Luther introduces himself.

- Theses 1–4 outline the underlying assumptions of the debate Luther wants to have.

- Thesis 5 states Luther's **primary thesis** about indulgences.

- This is followed in theses 6–80 by the **confirmation** or proof in which Luther seeks to confirm his primary thesis: theses 6–20 clarify the primary thesis; theses 21–40 reject the false claims of the indulgence preachers; theses 41–55 highlight the tension between preaching indulgences and encouraging Christians to do good works; theses 56–68 affirm that the treasure of the church is the gospel; and theses 69–80 outline how the church should respond.

- Theses 81–91 are the **confutation**, a rhetorical device in such academic disputations, in which the convention was to raises objections to your own thesis. As we shall see, in contrast Luther puts mischievous questions to the supporters of indulgences.

- Finally in theses 92–95 there is the **peroration** or conclusion in which, with a flourish, Luther rests his case.

**THESIS
1**

REFORMATIONAL CHRISTIANITY NEEDS TO BE NOURISHED BY REVERENT AND RIGOROUS THEOLOGICAL LEARNING

We begin with Luther's exordium or preface, in which he said:

> *Out of love for the truth and the desire to bring it to light, the following propositions will be discussed at Wittenberg, under the oversight of the Reverend Father Martin Luther, Master of Arts and Sacred Theology, & Lecturer on these subjects at Wittenberg.[11]*

Here we are reminded that the Reformation was born within a university. Luther was a professor and it was, as we've seen, through his study of the Bible – aided by the scholarship of Erasmus and others – that Luther came to understand what was wrong with the Roman Catholic penitential system and its understanding of the nature of salvation. Not surprisingly, therefore, in the years that followed, learning was highly prized by Lutherans and Calvinists across Europe and eventually across the world as classical Protestantism spread. Universities and theological academies were founded to ensure that churches had well-trained pastors and preachers. To take one example, English Puritans founded Emmanuel College in Cambridge for the training of godly ministers. One of its graduates was John Harvard, who emigrated to the Massachusetts Bay Colony where he left his library to a new college founded there in Cambridge, Massachusetts – and later renamed after him – in order to equip the instruction of godly ministers for the new world.

Today Reformational churches still need theological learning, and such learning must continue be reverent as well as rigorous. Of course there is – as there always was – a danger that learning becomes an end in itself or becomes worldly in seeking either cultural acceptance or academic respectability. Yet the antidote is not to shun learning but to ensure that it serves the churches in their mission to the world. Thus a priority – not the only one but a main one – must be the nurturing of theologians for both the lectern and the pulpit. In part that can be done in secular institutions, but far more important is to have flourishing centres of faithful theological learning that are accountable to churches. Pastors need to be well trained for ministry. While their spiritual life and the gaining of practical ministry skills are also essential, theological learning mustn't be neglected or worse despised. On the contrary reverent and rigorous theological learning must be a priority for Reformational churches.

What does this mean practically? It means that local churches need to be active in the provision of theological education. Some denominations or networks are very good at achieving this by formally sponsoring and financing training institutions. However, for many churches such support is almost non-existent. In the UK this may in part be due to the mistake of delegating such training to secular universities. Others welcome the enthusiastic amateur who can wing a sermon rather than seeking a preacher with suitable teaching, or, by embracing a hyperspirituality, expect the Holy Spirit alone to equip a person for everything. Another reason may be the inverted snobbery that says learning isn't necessary in order to minster to ordinary people. What needs to be recognised then is not only that we need academic training but also that such learning must fear God and be intellectually rigorous. For this reason churches or networks need to decide on the best way to train people for ministry in general and especially men for pastoral ministry in particular. Godly and gifted people need to be identified and then financially supported by churches, as well as being spiritually nurtured by older leaders. The training institutions they are sent to need to be well resourced.

AT THE HEART OF REFORMATIONAL CHRISTIANITY IS THE BIBLICAL DOCTRINE OF JUSTIFICATION BY FAITH ALONE, WHICH IS ESSENTIAL FOR A PROPER UNDERSTANDING OF THE GOSPEL AND ALL THAT MEANS IN BECOMING, LIVING AND DYING AS CHRISTIANS

To the surprise of many the doctrine of justification by faith alone is not mentioned in the 95 Theses. As we saw in the previous section it wasn't until two years later that

Luther had his doctrinal breakthrough for he dates that experience of first understanding the righteousness of God to the year he returned to lecturing on Romans in 1519. Clearly Luther's comprehension of this was developing before then but in 1517 it hadn't reached the point where he understood it to be the passive righteousness that is received by faith.

Nevertheless the seed of justification was in the 95 Theses and particularly thesis 1, which states:

> When our Lord and Master Jesus Christ said 'Repent,' he intended that the entire life of believers should be repentance.

Luther had come to see that penance as taught and practised by the church had nothing to do with repentance as revealed in Scripture. As he put it in his second thesis:

> The word repentance cannot be understood to mean the sacrament of penance, or the act of confession and satisfaction administered by the priests.

Rather than being an exercise of penitential discipline, repentance is the turning of the sinner to God for mercy from his or her sins, and that happens not once or occasionally in the life of a Christian but throughout their entire life. The reality of being a Christian is a lifelong struggle with sin and with Satan. As Luther was beginning to discover, the only basis on which such a struggle can be conducted is the passive righteousness of Christ that is received through faith alone. Only when united to Christ and clothed in his righteousness can a believer turn to God again and again from his or her sins, knowing that he or she will not be condemned but will be accepted and forgiven. Thus the entire life of believers needs to be one of repentance.

So it was that the seed sown in that first thesis grew to be the great oak tree of the Reformation's doctrine of justification, which is at the heart of Reformational Christianity. Later reformers – John Calvin, Thomas Cranmer and John Knox, to name but three – were at one with Luther when it came to justification. The Puritans in the 17th century were in agreement. In the 18th century George Whitefield, John Wesley and Jonathan Edwards preached Luther's doctrine to large crowds empowered by the Holy Spirit sent from heaven. It was this doctrine that was at the heart of the missionary endeavours of William Carey, Adoniram Judson, David Livingstone and Hudson Taylor plus many others in the 18th and 19th centuries, such as Thomas Chalmers and C.H. Spurgeon, who loved the doctrine of justification by faith alone. In the 20th century J. Gresham Machen, Martyn Lloyd-Jones, John Stott, J.I. Packer, Billy Graham and Francis Schaeffer loved, preached and taught the doctrine of justification. While not comprising the entire gospel, justification by faith alone is essential to a proper understanding of it and is indeed the doctrine by which the church stands or falls, as Luther later said.

In our own day we must not only confess this doctrine of justification, as eventually understood by Luther, but also preach it and appropriate it so that it is a living reality in our churches and lives. The problem is that, in large measure, this isn't the case. The late Richard Lovelace, a professor of church history in the United States, put his finger on what is wrong:

Only a fraction of the present body of professing Christians is solidly appropriating the justifying work of Christ in their lives. Many have so light an apprehension of God's holiness and of the extent and guilt of their sin that consciously they see little need for justification, although below the surface of their lives they are deeply guilt-ridden and insecure. Many others have a theoretical commitment to this doctrine, but in their day-to-day existence they rely on their sanctification for their justification ... drawing their assurance of acceptance with God from their sincerity, their past experience of conversion, their recent religious performance or the relative infrequency of their conscious, wilful disobedience. Few know enough to start each day with a thoroughgoing stand on Luther's platform: you are accepted, looking outward in faith and claiming the wholly alien [that is, outside of us] righteousness of Christ as the only ground for acceptance, relaxing in that quality of trust which will produce increasing sanctification as faith is active in love and gratitude.[12]

The spiritual health of Christianity is largely dependent on the degree to which what Lovelace describes is a reality. For this not to be the case justification by faith alone must be integral to preaching in church, pastoral care, evangelism, the way we conduct our relationships and much else. That doesn't mean that the language of justification has to be used as such; indeed doing so can be part of the problem if it becomes little more than theological box ticking. What is required is that the gospel in all its fullness becomes the heartbeat of the church and of every Christian. Together with John Bunyan, a great lover of Luther's writings, we must rejoice to see that our righteousness is at the right hand of the Father in Jesus Christ himself and that must shape all we think, do and say as Christians.

Furthermore we must be vigilant against all attacks on this doctrine, whether from old opponents or new. The most prevalent is our natural tendency to moralism – trying to please God by doing what's right without trusting in him for grace. For many of us this is our default position: just to try harder. Moralism can take numerous forms, whether it is that of the Catholicism of Luther's day (or of our day, for that matter) or of some Protestant version. Yet it always considers repentance as simply doing penance or us doing things to put ourselves right with God, rather than the genuine repentance that is the fruit of justifying faith. When that happens not only does our Christianity become drudgery and a joyless duty but we open ourselves to false teaching. Thinking that there must be more to being a Christian than this experience, we are tempted by false teachers that offer us more than the gospel.

The apostle Paul and others in the New Testament refuted such false teachers who said that there is something we can do, in addition to what Christ has done, that will justify us before God. But there are also many false teachers who would give us less than the gospel. For them the biblical doctrine of justification by faith, as

Luther understood it, is not an issue since it is outdated and should therefore be discarded. Such false teachers may talk much about grace but with little, if any, doctrine of sin, don't see why sinners need to be saved from God's wrath – which is offered by the death of Christ in their place on the cross.

UNBIBLICAL DOCTRINES AND PRACTICES IN CHURCHES THAT CONTRADICT OR UNDERMINE THE GOSPEL NEED TO BE CHALLENGED, REPUDIATED AND DISCARDED IF REFORMATIONAL CHRISTIANITY IS TO FLOURISH

What Luther was coming to discover in 1517 was that the marketing of indulgences was basically an attempt to sell and buy grace. So offended was he by this that he came to challenge, repudiate and discard it in the churches with which he had some influence. Here is how he stated the problem in thesis 5:

The pope does not intend to remit, and cannot remit, any penalties except those that he has imposed either by his own authority or by the authority of the canons.

We must remember that, at this point, Luther still accepted the authority of the pope and the place of penance and indulgences in the church. In fact in thesis 7 he said Christians must be in humble subjection to a priest, and in thesis 71 he pronounced an anathema against anyone who spoke against papal pardons. Then the problem on which he focused was the abuse of indulgences. But Luther was quickly coming to realise that the pope, penance and indulgences were all part of a system of religion that was antithetical to the gospel as revealed in Scripture. The direction in which his theology was developing is indicated in thesis 79:

To say that the cross emblazoned with the papal arms, which is set up by preachers of

> *indulgences, is of equal worth with the cross*
> *of Christ, is blasphemy.*

As Reformational Christians today we must challenge, repudiate and discard the similar doctrines and practices that contradict or undermine the gospel. One pernicious modern form of indulgences is the prosperity gospel, which is so widespread. The prosperity gospel says that if we believe, we can be materially prosperous and physically healthy. Whether seen in its softer (a nice life) or harder (more money) forms, it is still intrinsically an attempt to sell and buy grace. It must therefore be challenged as it fundamentally distorts the gospel, no matter how formally orthodox its proponents might seem. Liberal theology, which seeks to subtract from the Bible whatever is offensive to the dominant culture, also must be rejected. This theology has been destroying Protestant churches for almost two centuries and is basically moralistic in its insistence that people do what is right but without teaching a gospel of grace that will enable them to do so. Then, of course, there is the ongoing need to rebut the doctrines of Roman Catholicism and other forms of ritualistic Christianity that are fundamentally untouched by the Reformation, much as they may outwardly change in other ways.

But it is easy to throw stones at other people's houses. Are there things in our churches that can undermine the gospel of grace? Some churches can be very legalistic even as they confess and preach grace. For example, even if this is not intended, the message can be communicated that what it means to be a good Christian is less about our acceptance by God on the basis of what Christ has done and more about our acceptance by other people and our conformity to their standards of belief and behaviour. Or it may that our church gives the impression that the gospel is not for everyone who believes, but only for people of a certain race, class, age or culture. Or the issue in our church might be that regardless of what we formally believe the reality is that we live for the idols or God substitutes of our culture.

Two specific areas that I would especially like to highlight are those of pastoral care and our public worship. In the care that churches provide, Christian leaders need to make sure that at the heart of all they do is the gospel of grace. Reformational pastoral counselling is not sanctified self-help but the application to particular situations of the gospel of the God, who justifies and sanctifies sinners through faith. So marriage counselling, for example, should not simply be a vaguely Christianised version of what the world offers, even at its best, but rooted in our redemption in Jesus Christ. The same applies to every other area of life as well. It is so easy to tell people what to do without grounding what we say in grace. The other important area where we need to keep Luther's doctrine of justification at its heart is our public worship. Whether what we do together on Sunday or other occasions is traditional or contemporary in form, we need to ask ourselves if it is shaped by the gospel. That is about more than having hymns and songs that are biblical in content, but also thinking about, planning and leading public worship in the light of the gospel. Whatever manner they take, the liturgies of Reformational churches should tell the great story of salvation in such a way that exalts the Triune God and builds up his people before a watching world.

However it is important to add that we should be discerning and patient in challenging, repudiating and discarding those aspects of church life that could undermine the gospel. Luther himself picked his battles, though in a way that some might find difficult. For example, as mentioned before, during his enforced absence from Wittenberg, his colleague Andreas Karlstadt went further than Luther in removing images and introducing a vernacular service among other things. On his return Luther reversed the changes but he felt he couldn't force the pace of reform before people were ready for them. It was therefore years before he introduced the changes he wanted in the public worship in Wittenberg. Yet far more important to Luther was the doctrine preached in the pulpits, taught in the catechisms and expressed in the liturgy, and it was this on which he focused. Perhaps Luther was too cautious in his reforms but he was wise and had a pastoral heart. Many zealous Christians today would be wise to follow his example. Some things are non-negotiable as far as the gospel is concerned but many more are not. And in whatever we do we must act in love and humility and with courtesy. That is just as much a characteristic of Reformational Christianity.

THESIS 4

REFORMATIONAL CHRISTIANITY MUST BE CONCERNED FOR ORDINARY PEOPLE AND THEIR SPIRITUAL WELFARE

While born within a university context, Luther's concern about indulgences was no mere academic exercise. His concern was fundamentally pastoral. He was anxious for the spiritual welfare of the people he preached to in the Castle Church and lived among in Wittenberg. Two theses expressed this pastoral concern:

Every truly repentant Christian has a right to full remission of penalty and guilt, even without letters of pardon (thesis 36).

Every true Christian, whether living or dead, has part of all the benefits of Christ and the church; and this is granted to him by God, even without letters of pardon (thesis 37).

Indulgences were robbing ordinary people of what was rightfully theirs as Christians. All who truly repented were forgiven by God for their sins; it wasn't necessary to have an indulgence certificate. Luther's concern was further expressed in two related writings. The first was his letter to Albrecht of Mainz that he sent along with his 95 Theses on the same day he posted them. Here is part of what he said – he didn't mince his words:

O great God! In this way, excellent Father, souls committed to your care are being directed to death. A most severe reckoning has fallen on you above all others and is indeed growing. For that reason I could no longer keep silent about these things ... How ... can the [indulgence preachers] make the people secure and unafraid through those false tales and promises linked to indulgences, given that indulgences confer upon souls nothing of benefit for salvation or holiness but only remove external penalty, once commonly imposed by the [penitential] canons?[13]

Again we must remember that Luther was still in transition theologically and at this stage accepted the Catholic penitential system. Nevertheless we can see that pastoral concern motivated his protest.

Second, this is apparent in his *Sermon on Indulgences and Grace*, which is really a tract, and which he published in early 1518. Luther's 95 Theses had been written in Latin. Therefore, while they had been printed and distributed around Germany, they were not very accessible to the ordinary person. So Luther recast his arguments into vernacular German and a popular form that people could easily understand. It was an instant bestseller, being reprinted 24 times between 1518 and 1520.

For Luther that was only the beginning of the literature he wrote for the ordinary person. He was one of those theologians who could write learned treatises as well as simple books. An example of the latter is his little book on prayer written for his barber, Peter. Peter asked Luther one day for advice on how to pray, so Luther went off and wrote this wonderful guide. He told Peter that, like a good barber with his razor, he must first pay attention. Then Luther taught Peter how to take a phrase each day from the Apostles' Creed, Ten Commandments and Lord's Prayer, and to build his prayers around it. Likewise, Luther's Small and Large Catechisms distilled his teaching into a memorable form for families and churches.

Even as a preacher Luther aimed at ordinary people. When some of his academic colleagues complained that his sermons were too simple, he told them he was preaching not for them but for the maid at the back of the church. And what sermons they were! Read almost any of them and you can understand why people loved to listen to him. They were faithful to the text but full of life, colour and humour to bring the gospel to life.[14]

It should hardly need saying that Reformational Christianity today should be as concerned for the spiritual welfare of ordinary people as it has been at its best throughout history. Yes, we need reverent and rigorous theological learning, and therefore pastor-theologians, but we also need popular preachers with a passion to reach all kinds of people. It seems to me that in the UK the preaching that is common in many conservative evangelical churches has been developed to appeal predominately to their core members: younger, middle-class, professional people, who are neither charismatic nor Pentecostal. On one level there is nothing wrong with that, but there are many other people inside churches who need to be fed with the gospel and vast numbers outside churches who need to be converted. We need styles of preaching that reach a wide range of ordinary people with the gospel. We need popular preachers in our generation, just as Whitefield and Spurgeon were in theirs. Such preaching doesn't reject learning on the one hand or become sensationalist on the other. The best popular preaching is theologically well-informed and engages the mind as well as the will and emotions. What should drive us, as it drove Luther and even more so the Lord Jesus, is the desperate spiritual needs of ordinary people who so often are like sheep without a shepherd.

THESIS 5

IN REFORMATIONAL CHRISTIANITY CHRISTIANS SHOULD BE ENCOURAGED TO DO GOOD TO OTHERS BECAUSE THEY ARE SAVED BY GRACE, AND NOT IN ORDER TO EARN MERIT WITH GOD

One of Luther's concerns was that indulgences diverted money from the poor, who needed it, to the church, which could do without it.

Christians are to be taught that he who sees a man in need and passes him by and gives his money to pardons instead, purchases not the indulgences of the pope, but the indignation of God (thesis 45).

Christians should be taught that it would be the pope's wish, as it is his duty, to give of his own money to many of those from whom certain hawkers of pardons cajole money, even though the church of St. Peter might have to be sold (thesis 51).

That second thesis was somewhat wishful thinking on Luther's part, but we get his point. It would be far better in God's eyes for Christians to do good for the poor than spend hard-earned money on useless indulgences.

The importance of doing good works became a big theme in Luther's preaching and teaching. Contrary to what some people think, Luther was very concerned about how Christians live as well as with their relationship with God. However, while the Roman Catholic Church taught that good works won merit with God, Luther emphasised that they were the fruit of faith in their lives. This was the outworking of Luther's first thesis that 'the entire life of believers should be repentance'. In his *Lectures on Galatians*, of 1531–35, he put it this way:

When I have this [passive] righteousness within me, I descend from heaven like the rain that makes the earth fertile. That is, I come forth from another kingdom and I perform good works whenever the opportunity arises. If I am a minister of the word, I preach, I comfort the saddened, and I administer the sacraments. If I am a father, I rule my household and family, I train my children in piety and honesty. If I am a magistrate, I perform the office I have received by divine command. If I am a servant, I faithfully attend my master's affairs. In short, whoever knows for sure that Christ is his righteousness not only cheerfully and gladly works in his calling but also submits himself for the sake of love to magistrates, also their wicked laws, and to everything else in this present life – even, if need be, to burden and danger. For he knows that God wants this and that this obedience pleases him.[15]

No less than Luther stressed so, Reformational Christianity today must emphasise the doing of good works in the world in general and in the various callings in which Christians find themselves in particular. One of the great gifts of the Reformation was the recovery of the sacredness of everyday life. The work of a priest or pastor is not more holy than that of a housewife or farm labourer or merchant. Everyone is to live out their calling as Christians wherever God places them in life. All this is part of our progressive sanctification or transformation by grace and through faith. Indeed this is the emphasis of the New Testament, in which we are exhorted to offer our bodies 'as a living sacrifice' to God in view of his saving mercy to us in Christ (Romans 12:1) and to 'do good to all people, especially to those who belong to the family of believers' (Galatians 6:10).

More than great schemes of social change, this is how Christians can influence and even transform the world. In recent years there has been a welcome debate about the place of mercy or social ministries and public engagement by evangelical Christians. People have different arguments from the Bible for the position they advocate. But whatever the arguments, what cannot be disputed is that Christians are people saved by grace to do good works inside and outside the church. That can involve anything from helping a neighbour in some practical way to serving in public office. As the apostle Paul reminded Titus over and over again in his letter to him, as Christians we must learn to devote ourselves to doing good.

THESIS
6

THE WORD OF GOD AND THE PREACHING OF IT MUST BE CENTRAL TO THE LIFE OF THE CHURCH AND THE CHRISTIAN IN REFORMATIONAL CHRISTIANITY

In the years around 1517 Luther was deeply immersed in the Bible as he prepared his lectures. The effect was a growing conviction about three things: what was revealed in Scripture; the authority Scripture must have over the church; and the centrality it must have in the church's life through preaching. Not surprisingly Luther felt that indulgences threatened to supplant the word of God:

> They are the enemies of Christ and the pope who bid the Word of God to be silent in some church in order that pardons may be preached it others (thesis 53).

It is interesting from this thesis that Luther still had confidence that the pope was on his side. He continued:

> Injury is done to the Word of God when, in the same sermon, an equal or a longer time is spent on pardons than on the Word (thesis 54).

As time went on the Bible meant more and more to Luther. For him the life of the church was shaped by the word. He had a very strong doctrine of the word of God and its effectiveness. Therefore he understood that when God speaks, he accomplishes what he intends, be that in the Bible itself, in preaching or in the sacraments of baptism and the Lord's Supper.

Do we have that same confidence in God's word? The way many churches operate would seem to indicate that they don't. To be blunt, the word of God is not central to much that is done in them. In a lot of sermons today it may not be indulgences that supplant the word of God, but many other things can, such as an excessive number of anecdotes, opinions on an array of things, self-help advice or simply mishandling the text. Sadly much preaching is not expositional in nature, in that it does not explain and apply the message of the Bible. In contrast sermons often approach the text of Scripture thematically. While there can be a good place for this, the danger is that while such teaching may sound superficially biblical, in reality the conclusions it draws can be far from so. Especially when Bible verses are taken out of context, the text is twisted or distorted and a false gospel is preached. When that happens, the gospel is hidden, which is shameful. As Luther put it in his 62nd thesis:

The true treasure of the church is the most holy gospel of the glory and grace of God.

Luther was coming to discover that this treasure was not something that the church owned and could dispense with – through indulgences or anything else at a price. Rather it was something of which she was to be the faithful steward, through the ministry of the word and the sacraments of baptism and the Lord's Supper, and which she was to freely offer to people. Why this is so important is revealed by Luther in his *Explanations of the 95 Theses*, written shortly after they were posted but published later in 1518. As he stated:

> *According to the Apostle in Romans 1, the gospel is the preaching of the incarnate Son of God, given to us without any merit on our part for salvation and peace. It is a word of salvation, a word of grace, a word of comfort, a word of joy, a voice of the bridegroom and the bride, a good word, a word of peace ... Therefore the true glory of God springs from the gospel. At the same time we are taught that the law is fulfilled not by our works but by the grace of God who pities us in Christ and that it shall be fulfilled not through*

works but through faith, not by anything we
offer God, but by all we receive from Christ
and partake of him.[16]

If churches are to be Reformational, then
it is essential that the word of God and the
preaching of it is central to their lives. While
styles of preaching can vary greatly depending
on gifting, culture, temperament and other
things, Reformational preaching will, like
Luther's, be fundamentally expositional – as the
message of the gospel is explained and applied
from Scripture, so that Christ is proclaimed in
the power of the Spirit. But the centrality of the
word is not only about preaching. The whole
life of the church must be shaped by the Bible.
How this works out in practice has been much
debated by Protestants, but, whatever differences
there might be, the priorities and emphases of
Scripture must determine not only how and what
we preach, but also how we worship, evangelise,
care for one another and everything else. What
we should long for is a present-day rediscovery
of God's book, as happened in the reign of King
Josiah[17] and happened at the Reformation.

THESIS
7

IN THE FACE OF CHALLENGES AND OPPOSITION, ENTERPRISING CREATIVITY IS REQUIRED IN ADVANCING REFORMATIONAL CHRISTIANITY

Luther's 95 Theses – not so much what he said in them but rather what he did with them – revealed the enterprising creativity that would come to characterise his subsequent life and ministry. Remember that posting theses was a customary format for proposing an academic debate. Furthermore, as noted earlier, theses 81 to 91 are the confutation in which conventionally the proposer raises objections to his own argument. Luther turned this convention on its head. He introduced what Timothy Wengert calls 'a sharp lay person',[18] who rather than raising objections to Luther poses embarrassing and rather cheeky questions to the advocates of indulgences:

> Such questions as the following: 'Why does the pope not empty purgatory, for the sake of holy love and for the sake of desperate souls that are there, if he redeems an infinite number of souls for the sake of miserable money with which to build a church?' (thesis 82).

This was typical of Luther. He broke conventions left, right and centre. His style of preaching was unlike anything people had heard. In his sermons as well as writings he used his robust sense of humour both to expound Scripture but also to excoriate his opponents. He was also very enterprising in seeing the possibilities of the new printing technology in advancing the

Reformation cause. Wittenberg quickly became a publishing centre, with Luther's works at the top of bestsellers lists. In partnership with his friend Lucas Cranach, the younger Luther also developed and controlled the Luther brand as images of himself were sent all over Germany.[19] It wasn't simply by word of mouth that the Reformation spread so fast and so widely.

Contemporary Reformational Christians need to learn from Luther. One of the biggest technological breakthroughs in our times, comparable to the invention of the printing press, is the Internet. Happily, many Reformational Christians, churches and ministries are utilising it to advance the kingdom of Christ. Search the Internet and you can find vast amounts of excellent Reformational resources that are easily accessible in a way unthinkable in previous generations. While the Internet contains much spiritual rubbish it therefore also contains great spiritual riches. But there are other ways that people are being creatively enterprising for the gospel. One example is the way catechising is being adapted to contemporary contexts such as housing estates. Another is the multiplication of ministry apprenticeship schemes for training a larger number and wider range of people for gospel ministry. Still others are the fresh approaches to church planting and revitalisation. The kingdom of Christ advances today, as it always has done, by the prayerful preaching of God's word, but that doesn't rule out, as it didn't in Luther's day, some enterprising creativity as well.

THESIS 8

REFORMATIONAL CHRISTIANITY REQUIRES NOT THEOLOGIANS AND PREACHERS OF GLORY BUT THEOLOGIANS AND PREACHERS OF THE CROSS OF CHRIST

Near the end of his 95 Theses Luther hinted at a theme that would become an important one to him and that is the contrast in what is taught between theologians of glory and theologians of the cross:

Away, then, with all those prophets who say to the people of Christ, 'Peace, peace,' and there is no peace! (thesis 92)

Echoing the words of the prophet Jeremiah,[20] Luther accused the preachers of indulgences of offering people a false peace, which means, of course, that they have no true peace with God. Rather, what is needed is the preaching of the cross of Christ:

Blessed be all those prophets who say to the people of Christ, 'Cross, cross,' and there is no cross! (thesis 93)

The cross of Christ would become central to Luther's theology and preaching. The problem with the preachers of indulgences was that they offered people glory without suffering, both their own suffering and that of Christ. By paying some money for an indulgence they claimed a person could escape suffering and didn't even need the suffering of Christ. Luther, though, came increasingly to understand that salvation was not to be found in the glorious or outwardly impressive things to which people were likely to look and trust in, such as indulgences, but in the cross of Christ. Echoing the words of Paul in 1 Corinthians 1 and 2, it was in the hiddenness, foolishness and weakness of the cross of Christ that God supremely revealed himself. It was in what God did in sending his Son to die for sinners on the cross that the punishment for sin was removed from those who believe. Thus for them there is 'no cross' – there is no punishment for sin to suffer.

If Reformational Christianity is to be recovered, what is needed are unashamed preachers of the cross of Christ. How easy it is for us to want glory as the world understands it rather than the cross. The recent controversy about the penal substitutionary nature of atonement illustrates the problem. No one who calls himself an evangelical will deny the importance of the death of Christ, but some are denying that Jesus bore the punishment of our sins because such an idea is despised by the culture. In this way they have become theologians and preachers of glory rather than of the cross. Reformational Christians must resist such temptations and keep the cross central in preaching, teaching, evangelism, discipleship and pastoral care, as well as in our own day-to-day lives.

THESIS
9

REFORMATIONAL CHRISTIANITY DEMANDS COSTLY DISCIPLESHIP

Having spoken about his cross, Jesus called on those who would be his disciples to deny themselves, take up their cross and follow him.[21] For Luther such discipleship was the essence of the Christian life and was costly:

Christians are to be exhorted to be diligent in following Christ, their Head, through penalties, death, and hell (thesis 94).

And thus be confident of entering into heaven through many tribulations, rather than through the false assurance of peace (thesis 95).

In this life Christians should expect afflictions and suffering, as the Bible makes abundantly clear. This is contrary to the false gospel of the indulgence preachers of Luther's day and the prosperity and positive-thinking preachers of our day. Indeed, sadly we can all shy away from the costliness of following Jesus.

Dietrich Bonhoeffer, the German pastor famous for protesting against the Nazis, also needed to confront the culturally comfortable Lutheranism of his day. These words of his echo Luther: 'Cheap grace is the preaching of forgiveness without requiring repentance, baptism without church discipline, Communion without confession, absolution without personal confession.'

Yet while true discipleship is costly, by contrast the grace of the gospel is costly even though it is wonderfully free. As Robert Kolb and Charles Arand say: '[Grace] cost Christ his life; it costs the sinner his or her very existence as sinner; it costs the believer the burden, pain and deprivation of bearing the cross of Christ in order to love the neighbour.'[22]

Reformational Christianity must not and cannot shrink from or hide the costliness of following Jesus. Being a Christian is not about enhancing our lifestyle with a bit of spiritual meaning and purpose. It is easy to let the comfort, security (financial and otherwise) and pleasure that the world says are rightfully ours control our lives rather than the Lord Jesus Christ. But Jesus demands that we deny ourselves and take up our cross and follow him. Like a seed, each of us must fall into the ground and die in order to bear fruit.

As Christianity becomes increasingly counter-cultural, the costly nature of true discipleship must be emphasised. Salvation is totally free and by grace, but it will cost us everything. Luther understood that; so must we.

THESIS
9.5

WHILE ACTION MUST BE TAKEN IN ADVANCING REFORMATIONAL CHRISTIANITY, WE MUST NOT FORGET THE ROLE OF GOD'S PROVIDENCE AND PRAYER IN ACCOMPLISHING HIS SAVING PURPOSES IN HISTORY

I admit that having 9.5 and not 10 theses is something of a gimmick, but it is one of which I like to think Luther would have approved. God's providence and prayer merit only half a point not because they are minor subjects but because they are not mentioned in the 95 Theses. Many other things could be discussed, but it is providence and prayer that I want to mention in closing since the impact of the 95 Theses can't be explained without reference to them.

First, that the theses sparked the Reformation is an amazing testimony to God's providential activity in history. In 1517 Luther didn't intend the Reformation to happen, but it did. As he claimed later in life, he did nothing whereas God's word did it all:

Take me, for example. I opposed indulgences and all papists, but never by force. I simply taught, preached, wrote God's Word: otherwise I did nothing. And then, while I slept or drank Wittenberg beer with my Philip and Amsdorf the Word so greatly weakened the papacy that never a prince or emperor did such damage to it. I did nothing: the Word did it all. Had I wanted to start trouble ... I could have started such a little game at Worms that even the emperor wouldn't have been safe. But what would it have been? A mug's game. I did nothing: I left it to the Word.[23]

However, the advance of the Reformation was not quite as simple as that. God did indeed work powerfully by his Spirit through the preaching of the word, but he also providentially ordered things in such a way that the Reformation spread like wildfire.

As we think of our own situation today, we would do well to remember this. Troubling as our world is, our God is providentially in control of all that is happening. Recent history bears witness to how the gospel has advanced and continues to do so in the most unlikely places and circumstances. We need only think of the growth of Christianity in sub-Saharan Africa or China or the growth of Protestantism in Latin America. But what about the contrasting situation here in Europe? We are called to be faithful and prayerful as we wait patiently for God to work in his way – according to his timescale and not ours. Confidence in God's providential activity is not an excuse for us to do nothing, but rather is reassurance that our efforts are not in vain as God weaves them into the tapestry of his unfolding purposes in the world.

This brings us to our second point: the role of prayer. Though it is not seen in the 95 Theses, we need to remember that Luther was as much a man of prayer as he was a theologian, preacher and church leader. Memorably Luther's friend and colleague Philip Melancthon said this about him:

> No day passes that he does not give three hours to prayer, and those the fittest for study. Once I happened to hear him. Good God! How great a spirit, how great faith, was in his very words! With such reverence did he ask, as if he felt he was speaking with God; with such hope and faith, as with a father and a friend.[24]

Yet sadly it is often those Christians who think they are loyal to the Reformation heritage who are not as devoted to prayer as they should be. Committed as we are to the ministry of the word, we must also be committed to the ministry of prayer – as has been the case with all men and women whom God has used to advance his kingdom. Such praying is not about complicated or demanding devotional disciplines, but, as the

Scottish reformer John Knox put it, about 'an earnest and familiar talking with God'.[25] The advance of Reformational Christianity in our generation requires a passionate commitment to prayer.

So we must have both a confidence in God's providential activity in the world and a commitment to prayer. Then we can be confident that God is at work in small events and ordinary lives to advance his saving purposes in this world. We tend to look back at what happened in the wake of 1517 and see the Reformation as a mighty movement of God. And so it was. But that movement involved ordinary people being faithful to Christ in the ordinary circumstances of their lives. That's what happened with Martin Luther in 1517, and that is what continues to happen today. The challenge to us is to be faithful to Christ and his gospel in our circumstances, and to leave the rest to God.

POSTSCRIPT

What happened in Wittenberg sometime on 31 October 1517 changed the world and continues to impact our lives today. I trust that by recasting Luther's 95 Theses as 9.5 Theses you have seen how significant they are for Christianity nowadays. Yet there are many who would like us to think that the Reformation doesn't really matter anymore.

The Roman Catholic Church certainly would, but there are many Protestants who think the same. They say that whatever our views on justification, it is not worth dividing the church over the issue. Faced with the problems there are in the world, and not least increasing hostility to Christianity in the West, they argue we need to stand together. In the light of that, they maintain that the historic concerns of Protestants about some Roman Catholic beliefs and practices need to be kept in perspective. At worst they are aberrations no different than some Protestant idiosyncrasies, and at best may have something to them. While admitting the Reformation had some benefits for the church and the world, they see it as a tragedy that shouldn't have happened. Indeed they contend that some of the worst aspects of the modern world – excessive individualism or secularism, to take two examples often cited – can be blamed on the Reformation, as can the denominational confusion of contemporary Protestantism. It's not surprising then that many Protestants and some evangelicals want to, and some even do, go over to 'the other side'.

However, those who are committed to the teaching of the Bible about salvation by grace think that the Reformation was necessary and really does matter. This is not only because in many things the teaching and practice of the Roman Catholic Church is still out of line with Scripture, but also because there is much in Protestantism that still needs reforming. The Bible is very clear how easily the visible people of God can revert to their bad old ways after significant advances of God's kingdom. Unbiblical doctrines and practices can take hold in churches. Even in Reformational churches for which the 9.5 Theses we've been thinking about are in some measure true, the Reformational heritage needs to be constantly renewed. Being a Reformational church is about more than formally adhering to the core principles of the Reformation; it is also about rejoicing in those principles and letting them transform the lives of God's people as the Holy Spirit demonstrates the power of the gospel.

Therefore Reformational Christians and churches must commit themselves afresh to the gospel of God's saving grace in Jesus Christ that Luther and other reformers rediscovered in the 16th century. We must preach it in dependence on the Holy Spirit as we strive to live it out in our lives. Of course there are many things not essential to salvation about which we do not agree. Reformational Christianity will always be expressed in a multitude of different ways. Nevertheless we can be united in the essentials of the gospel and work together to see that gospel is spread through the nations as it is made known. That great work begins with each of us and in every local congregation of Christians. The Reformation as a movement of personal and corporate spiritual renewal happened because the saving power of the gospel changed the lives of ordinary people from well-known individuals, like Luther, to the maid at the back of the church where he preached or the plough boy William Tyndale had in mind when he began to translate the Bible into English. In the same way what happened in the 16th century continues to happen today as lives are transformed by the gospel. Of course our world is very different in a myriad of ways from that of Luther in Wittenberg in 1517. Not least is the fact that the centre of gravity of Christianity has shifted towards Africa and Asia. But the Reformation gospel, which is the gospel of the Bible, is as powerful as ever and in the end will accomplish God's purpose to bring salvation by his Son to the ends of the earth.

REFERENCES

[1] Just as I began to put my research into the form of the paper I gave at the Westminster Conference in 2016 I came across an article from 2012 by Carl Trueman entitled '9.5 Theses on Martin Luther Against the Self-Indulgences of the Modern Church'. I happily concede that Prof. Trueman came up with the idea of 9.5 theses first, although he takes them in a different direction than I do. The article can be found on the Reformation 21 website at http://www. reformation21.org/articles/95-theses-on-martin-luther-against-the-selfindulgences-of-the-modern-church.php

[2]   For an accessible introduction to the
      Reformation 'solas' see Terry L. Johnson,
      The Case for Traditional Protestantism
      (Edinburgh: Banner of Truth Trust, 2004).
      For a more academic approach see Kevin
      J. Vanhoozer, *Biblical Authority after Babel*
      (Grand Rapids, Michigan: Brazos Press,
      2016). For group Bible study see Jason
      Helopoulos, *These Truths Alone* (Epsom,
      Surrey: Good Book Company, 2017).

Part 1: A short overview of Martin Luther's life

[3]   The classic biography of Luther and still
      one of the best is Roland H. Bainton's *Here
      I Stand: A Life of Martin Luther* (Tring, Herts:
      Lion Publishing, 1978). The most recent
      large-scale biography is Lyndall Roper's
      Martin Luther: Renegade and Prophet (London:
      Bodley Head, 2016). For a good introduction
      to Luther's life and theology see Stephen J.
      Nichols, *Martin Luther: A Guided Tour of His
      Life and Thought* (Phillipsburg, New Jersey:
      P&R Publishing, 2002).

4   Lyndal Roper, *Martin Luther*, p. 205.

5   Stephen J. Nichols, *Martin Luther*, p. 8.

6   Timothy J. Wengert, *Martin Luther's Ninety-Five Theses* (Minneapolis: Fortress Press, 2015), pp. xv–xxi.

7   Timothy J. Wengert, *Martin Luther's Ninety-Five Theses*, p. xxix.

8   Lyndal Roper, *Martin Luther*, p. 3.

9   Roland Bainton, *Here I Stand*, p. 65.

Part 2: My 9.5 Theses for the recovery of Reformational Christianity

10   Timothy J. Wengert, *Martin Luther's Ninety-Five Theses*, pp. 7–8.

11   The translation of the 95 Theses I use is that of Stephen J. Nichols, *Martin Luther*, pp. 21–47.

12   Richard L. Lovelace, *Dynamics of Spiritual Renewal* (Illinois: IVP and Buckinghamshire: Paternoster Press, 1979), pp. 101.

13   Timothy J. Wengert, *Martin Luther's Ninety-Five Theses*, pp. 33–34.

14 For a fascinating insight in Luther's use of biblical narrative in preaching see Robert Kolb, *Luther and the Stories of God* (Grand Rapids: Baker Academic, 2012).

15 Cited by Robert Kolb and Charles P. Arand, *The Genius of Luther's Theology* (Grand Rapids: Baker Academic, 2008), p. 101.

16 Martin Luther, *Explanations of the Ninety-Five Theses, in Luther's Works* (Minneapolis: Fortress Press and St Louis: Concordia Press, 1957), vol. 31, p. 57.

17 See 2 Kings 22:8. As a result of this discovery, Josiah read the Book of the Law in the hearing of all the people and then renewed their covenant with God, in which they promised to follow him and keep all his commands (2 Kings 23:1–3).

18 Timothy J. Wengert, *Martin Luther's Ninety-Five Theses,* p. 8.

19 Andrew Pettegree, *Brand Luther* (London: Penguin, 2015), pp. 78–83. See also 'The Great Reformers', Apollo Magazine, October 2016.

[20] See Jeremiah 6:14; 8:11.

[21] See Mark 8:34.

[22] Robert Kolb and Charles P. Arand, *The Genius of Luther's Theology*, p. 92, where the Bonhoeffer quotation can also be found.

[23] Cited in James Atkinson, *Martin Luther and the Beginning of the Reformation* (Harmondsworth, Middlesex: Penguin, 1968), p. 182.

[24] Cited in James Atkinson, *Martin Luther and the Beginning of the Reformation*, p. 250.

[25] John Knox, *Select Practical Writings of John Knox* (Edinburgh: Free Church of Scotland, 1845), p. 31.

a division of **10** of those.com

10Publishing is the publishing house of **10ofThose**.
It is committed to producing quality Christian
resources that are biblical and accessible.

www.10ofthose.com is our online retail arm selling
thousands of quality books at discounted prices.

For information contact: **info@10ofthose.com**
or check out our website: **www.10ofthose.com**